Acting Up!

A Lillenas Drama Resource

with 12 comedy scripts for teens

by Doug Smee

Lillenas Publishing Company
Kansas City, MO 64141

Copyright © 1991
by Lillenas Publishing Company

All rights reserved

Printed in the United States of America

Amateur performance rights are granted when two copies of this work are purchased.

After the two copies are purchased, you may duplicate individual sketch scripts from this book for $1.00 per copy—$10.00 maximum payment per individual sketch. Note: This applies only to sketches and monologues.

Please include the following on each reproduced copy:

From "Acting Up!"
Copyright © 1991 by Lillenas Publishing Co.
All rights reserved
Used with permission, Lillenas Publishing Co.

Repro rights are granted upon the receipt of your check with this information included:

1. Title, source, and author(s) of script(s)
2. Number of copies per sketch

Mail your request and check to:

Lillenas Drama Resources
Copyright Permission Desk
P.O. Box 419527
Kansas City, MO 64141

Cover art by Paul Franitza

Unless otherwise indicated, all Scripture quotations are taken from *The Holy Bible, New International Version*, copyright © 1973, 1978, 1984 by the International Bible Society, and are used by permission.

Scripture quotation marked NASB is from the *New American Standard Bible* (NASB), © The Lockman Foundation, 1960, 1962, 1963, 1968, 1971, 1972, 1973, 1975, 1977, and is used by permission.

King James Version (KJV)

Dedication

Since my last book, the Lord has seen fit to free a very special woman and one of His true disciples from the pain and suffering of this world. I will not try to list the Christian qualities of my mother. Let me simply say that in my life as a parent, teacher, and Christian, if I ever have a question about what I should do, I can simply ask, "What would Harriet Smee do?"

I dedicate this book to her, not because I miss her, but because she loved laughter and the Lord more than anything else in this world.

"Her children rise up and bless her; her husband also, and he prasies her. . . . Charm is deceitful and beauty is vain, but a woman who fears the Lord, she shall be praised."
—Proverbs 31:28, 30, NASB

Contents

Love of Another Kind 9

God's Help 14

Helpers 19

The Invitation 22

The Cure 27

The Gifts 31

The Pharisee and Publicity 34

Where Angels Fear to Tread 39

Blind Bart 43

Behold and Beware 48

A Funny Thing Happened 53

You Were There 57

Love of Another Kind

This is probably the easiest of the skits in this book. There is a minimum of props, and no special costumes are needed. The actors can concentrate on their actions, since they can hold their scripts. I wrote "Love..." for three of the young ladies in my drama troupe. However, the gender of the parts can be changed easily. A great deal of the comedy in this skit depends on how much the actors ham up their parts. Also, they should try to repeat the exact same motions and intonations in each take of their reunion scene.

Theme

"How great is the love the Father has lavished on us, that we should be called children of God! And that is what we are! The reason the world does not know us is that it did not know him" (1 John 3:1).

Scripture

Luke 15:11-24

Cast

DIRECTOR
MOTHER
DAUGHTER

Props

Three Scripts
Director's Chair
Bible

(Enter MOTHER, DAUGHTER, and DIRECTOR *with scripts in hand.*)

DIRECTOR *(spoken to imaginary crew):* All right, boys and girls, let's get this last scene ready to go. We can get this puppy in the can by lunch. *(To* MOTHER *and* DAUGHTER*)* OK, let's run through this once with the scripts. Are you ready?

MOTHER: Julian, darling, I wonder if you could run through the story to this point? It would help me get in touch with my motivation for this scene.

DIRECTOR: Anything for you, Babe. The rotten daughter . . .

DAUGHTER: That's me.

DIRECTOR: . . . has demanded of her loving mother . . .

MOTHER: That's me.

DIRECTOR: . . . her share of the mother's fortune. She has taken the money and spent it foolishly.

DAUGHTER: I thought the characters were originally a father and son.

DIRECTOR: I know, but Sweetie, Sugar, Baby, we want to give it a new look. Besides, Dustin and Tom wouldn't sign.

MOTHER: So what has happened just before this scene?

DIRECTOR: The wayward daughter . . .

DAUGHTER: That's me.

DIRECTOR: . . . after ruining her life, returns to her mother . . .

MOTHER: That's me.

DIRECTOR: . . . to ask for forgiveness. This scene is that touching reunion. Are we ready? Great! You're all beautiful! Let's do it! *(Moves stage right)* This is "Love of Another Kind," Scene 25, Take 1 . . . and action!!

(Both MOTHER *and* DAUGHTER *ham it up and overact.)*

DAUGHTER: Dear Mother, I have come home . . .

MOTHER: Can that truly be you, dear daughter?

DAUGHTER: Yes, Mother. I have returned from my foolish journeys.

MOTHER *(harshly):* Well, you can just go back where you came from, honey!

DAUGHTER *(looks frantically through the script):* What??

MOTHER: You heard me. I don't want to see your ugly face around here anymore!

DAUGHTER *(looks helplessly toward* DIRECTOR*):* Julian? Julian? I'm lost. Where is she getting these lines?

DIRECTOR *(moves back to center stage):* Cut! *(To* DAUGHTER*)* Take it easy, I'll find out. *(To* MOTHER*)* Sweetie, Sugar, Baby, what's happening? That's not in the script.

MOTHER: Julian, darling, I'm a method actress. I have to imagine what my character would be feeling, and then act it out. You can't tell me that this mother would be happy to welcome this bratty kid home.

DIRECTOR: Sweetie, Sugar, Baby, that's the way the script is written.

MOTHER: But, Julian, darling, it doesn't make sense.

DIRECTOR: I know, dear, but let's try it whether it makes sense or not.

MOTHER *(sighs):* If you say so, Julian.

DIRECTOR: That's great. Love ya. *(Moves stage right)* "Love of Another Kind," Scene 25, Take 2 . . . and action!

DAUGHTER: Dear Mother, I have come home . . .

MOTHER: Can that truly be you, dear daughter?

DAUGHTER: Yes, Mother. I have returned from my foolish journeys.

MOTHER: Yes . . . uh . . . what do you want?

DAUGHTER: I know that I have sinned against God and against you. I am not worthy to be called your daughter. I have come home only to be *(kneeling dramatically)* your servant.

MOTHER *(puts hand on* DAUGHTER's *shoulder):* You shall not be a servant.

DAUGHTER: You mean you forgive me and accept me as your daughter?

MOTHER: No way!! I wouldn't have you for my watchdog! Why, I should—

DIRECTOR: Cut!! Cut!! *(Moves back to center stage)*

DAUGHTER: Julian, I can't take much more of this!

DIRECTOR *(to* DAUGHTER*):* I know, Baby, you've been great. Just take a breather. I'll take care of everything. *(To* MOTHER*)* Sweetie, Sugar, Baby, that's not what the script says. The mother loves her daughter and wants her back home.

MOTHER: But Julian, darling, I don't understand. Surely this kid deserves a good swat, at least. Maybe even—

DIRECTOR *(keeping his temper with great effort; through teeth):* Sweetie, Sugar, Baby. Do it the way it's written, with love. *(Gets louder and louder)* I don't want punishment! I don't want revenge!! I don't want anger!!! I WANT LOVE!!! DO YOU UNDERSTAND?? LOVE!!

MOTHER: Yes, Julian.

DIRECTOR *(under control again):* Great. Wonderful. You're beautiful. *(Moves stage right)* "Love of Another Kind," Scene 25, Take 3 . . . and action!

DAUGHTER: Dear Mother, I have come home . . .

MOTHER: Can that truly be you, dear daughter?

DAUGHTER: Yes, Mother. I have returned from my foolish journeys.

MOTHER: Yes . . . uh . . . so you have.

DAUGHTER: I know that I have sinned against God and against you. I am not worthy to be called your daughter. I have come home only to be *(kneeling dramatically)* your servant.

MOTHER *(puts hand on DAUGHTER's shoulder):* You shall not be a servant.

DAUGHTER: You mean you forgive me and accept me as your daughter?

MOTHER *(sigh):* I guess so.

DAUGHTER: Oh, thank you, dear mother. *(Stands and spreads arms to hug MOTHER)* I don't deserve your love and forgiveness. I—

MOTHER *(breaking in):* Well, I'm glad you are finally showing some sense.

DAUGHTER *(starts to look frantically through script):* Oh, no. Not again.

MOTHER: But before you come one step into my house, I have a few, well-chosen words to say to you about what you've done, you worthless, little—

DIRECTOR *(screaming):* Cut!! Cut!! *(Moves back to center stage)*

DAUGHTER *(to DIRECTOR):* Julian? I just can't work with this. I'm going back to my trailer. *(Looks scornfully toward MOTHER)* Give me a call when you get Mother straightened out. *(Exit DAUGHTER)*

DIRECTOR *(calling after DAUGHTER):* I'll take care of it. You were beautiful. Let's do lunch, soon. Have your people call my people. *(To MOTHER, getting louder with each word)* Sweetie. Sugar! Baby!! WHAT DO YOU THINK YOU'RE DOING?

MOTHER: But, Julian, even if I loved her enough to accept her back, doesn't she need to know how rotten she's been?

DIRECTOR *(in control—barely):* That's not the way this mother works. She loves her daughter more than that. She doesn't want to reject her, punish her, or make her feel worthless. She just wants to love her.

MOTHER *(throwing up hands):* I'm afraid I just can't get in touch with that kind of love.

DIRECTOR: I see. *(Taking Bible)* Sweetie, Sugar, Baby. I think it's time we went over the original script. *(As* MOTHER *and* DIRECTOR *exit)* This is a good place to start: "For God so loved the world . . ."

God's Help

This is probably my favorite skit, because it was the first I ever wrote. Since I wrote it in 1976, I have probably performed it more than any other. This was inspired by the give-and-take seen in the great comedic duos, like Abbott and Costello. The pace should not slacken. The two actors should find a way to insert their own personality into this skit.

Theme

"What, then, shall we say in response to this? If God is for us, who can be against us?" (Romans 8:31).

Scripture

1 Samuel 17

Cast

ACTOR 1
ACTOR 2

Props

Sack of Cookies

(Enter ACTOR 1, *who moves to center stage with great enthusiasm.*)

ACTOR 1: Do we have a story for you today! But first . . . *(looking around)* . . . I'm going to need some help.

(Enter ACTOR 2, *concentrating on eating a cookie from his sack.* ACTOR 1 *grabs him as he comes by.*)

ACTOR 1: How about you? Will you help me?

ACTOR 2 *(mouth full)*: Mumble mumble?

ACTOR 1: Thank you for volunteering. You're a good sport.

(ACTOR 1 *slaps* ACTOR 2 *on back, causing him to swallow and cough and choke a little.*)

ACTOR 1: First, we won't need these.

(ACTOR 1 *takes* ACTOR 2's *bag of cookies and tosses it to stage left.*)

ACTOR 2: Wait! Those are my cookies!

ACTOR 1: Relax. They're not good for you anyway. Let's begin by asking you a few questions. Can you tell us why you come to church?

ACTOR 2: Well . . . uh . . . *(Looks longingly after cookies)* I like church, I guess.

ACTOR 1: That's fine. But why do you like church?

ACTOR 2 *(still staring at bag)*: Uh . . . let's see . . . I guess because I love God.

ACTOR 1: That's nice. But can you tell us why you love God?

ACTOR 2 *(looks from bag to* ACTOR 1 *and back again)*: Are any of these questions multiple choice?

ACTOR 1: Well, you could say that God is good, or that He loves you, or that He helps you every day.

ACTOR 2: Fine. *(Starting for bag)* I say all of the above.

ACTOR 1 *(stopping* ACTOR 2 *and bringing him back to center stage)*: How about an answer of your own?

ACTOR 2: What??

ACTOR 1: For instance, how does God help you?

ACTOR 2: OK. . . . uh . . . He . . . uh . . . *(Looking at bag)* . . . He makes cookies. *(Starts for bag again)*

ACTOR 1 *(stopping* ACTOR 2 *and bringing him back to center stage)*: Hold on! God makes cookies?

ACTOR 2 *(patiently)*: Sure! You see, without God there would be no oats for oatmeal cookies.

ACTOR 1: Oh, I think I understand. . . .

ACTOR 2: Without God there'd be no chocolate for chocolate chip cookies.

ACTOR 1 *(to audience)*: You know, he's right?

ACTOR 2 *(violently)*: And without God there'd be no me to eat the cookies! *(Starts for bag again)*

ACTOR 1 *(stopping ACTOR 2 and bringing him back to center stage)*: So you see that God helps you in making cookies?

ACTOR 2: Yes!! Now may I go? *(Starts for bag again)*

ACTOR 1 *(stopping ACTOR 2 and bringing him back to center stage)*: Not quite yet.

ACTOR 2 *(looking to heaven)*: What have I done??

ACTOR 1: You know God helped many people throughout the Bible.

ACTOR 2 *(looking to heaven)*: I could use some help now.

ACTOR 1: And He helped with more important things than cookies. How about that little boy named David?

ACTOR 2: What about him?

ACTOR 1: Let's tell that story together. You know it, don't you?

ACTOR 2: Sure. *(Looks toward bag again)* If I help you tell this story, can I go?

ACTOR 1: Of course.

ACTOR 2: Great! OK. Let's go.

ACTOR 1: David was a boy—

ACTOR 2: And he lived happily ever after. The end. *(Starts for bag again)*

ACTOR 1 *(stopping ACTOR 2 and bringing him back to center stage)*: Wait a minute. Let's do this right.

ACTOR 2 *(shaking head)*: Oh, boy.

ACTOR 1: David was a boy not much bigger than some of these boys right here. *(Points to audience)*

ACTOR 2: Kind of puny, wasn't he.

ACTOR 1: Watch it!

ACTOR 2: Sorry.

ACTOR 1: Anyway, David had to run an errand for his father Jesse—

ACTOR 2 *(getting wild)*: Jesse James! Bang! bang! bang! bang!

ACTOR 1: No, no! Just plain Jesse.

ACTOR 2: Sorry. I'm going through sugar withdrawal.

ACTOR 1: David had to take a picnic lunch to his brothers who were in the army of Israel.

ACTOR 2 *(looks at bag)*: Lots of cookies, I suppose?

ACTOR 1: I suppose so.

ACTOR 2: Sigh.

ACTOR 1: Anyway, when David arrived at the battlefield, do you know what he saw?

ACTOR 2: Sure! It was a big, ugly, smelly, 29-foot . . . midget!!

ACTOR 1: Giant!! It was a giant!!

ACTOR 2: I know. I was just testing.

ACTOR 1: Oh, yeah? Do you know the name of the giant?

ACTOR 2: Uh . . . let's see . . . Was he green and always saying, "Ho, ho, ho"?

ACTOR 1: No! *(To kids in the audience)* Do you know? That's right. Goliath. And Goliath was 9 feet tall, not 29 feet.

ACTOR 2: That's still pretty big to me.

ACTOR 1 *(patting* ACTOR 2's *stomach)*: It looks like you're trying to catch up.

ACTOR 2: Just tell the story.

ACTOR 1: Goliath was bigger and stronger than anybody in the army of Israel. He was also challenging anyone to come and fight him, but nobody would.

ACTOR 2: I don't blame them.

ACTOR 1: But David said, "I'll fight the giant!"

ACTOR 2 *(pause)*: Not only was he puny, but he was a little dumb too.

ACTOR 1: No. David knew that God would help him and protect him. So he wasn't scared to fight the giant. So he went down to a stream and picked up five smooth stones—

ACTOR 2: Stones??

ACTOR 1: That's right. For his slingshot.

ACTOR 2: Slingshot!! Man, I wouldn't get into this unless I had a sword, spear, shield, and 35-millimeter bazooka!

ACTOR 1: David was too small to use any of those weapons, and besides, he was a crack shot with his slingshot.

ACTOR 2 *(acting out a quick draw)*: Fastest slingshot in the West!

ACTOR 1 (*looking and pointing up.* ACTOR 2 *also looks up*): Here comes the giant . . . shaking the earth as he walks . . . (ACTOR 2 *starts vibrating as if the earth is shaking*) . . . screaming that he's going to squash David like a fly . . . (ACTOR 2's *eyes get wider and wider*) . . . He throws his spear!!

ACTOR 2 (*ducking behind* ACTOR 1): AHHH!!

ACTOR 1 (*dryly*): Thanks a lot.

ACTOR 2 (*peeking from behind*): Better you than me.

ACTOR 1: He missed.

ACTOR 2 (*stepping out*): Whew. That was close. (*Pointing behind them*) Got my camel, though. Yuck! Camel shish kebab!

ACTOR 1 (*looking up*): Give me strength.

(ACTOR 2 *continues to act out the story as* ACTOR 1 *tells it.*)

ACTOR 1: David puts a stone into his slingshot and winds up. . . . He shoots the stone . . .

ACTOR 2: Zoooom!!

ACTOR 1: It hits Goliath right between the eyes!

ACTOR 2: Bingo!!

ACTOR 1: The giant falls!!

ACTOR 2: Ti-im-m-ber-r-r!!

ACTOR 1: David beats Goliath, and the Israelites win the battle!

ACTOR 2: Hooray!! (*Runs and gets bag*) Cookies for everyone!! (*Eats a cookie*)

ACTOR 1: That was a good story about God's help, wasn't it?

ACTOR 2: It sure was. I especially liked the ending. (*Eats another cookie*)

ACTOR 1: That's good. Let's try another story. Once, there was a man named—

(ACTOR 2 *quickly takes a cookie and stuffs it into* ACTOR 1's *mouth. He then pushes* ACTOR 1 *offstage as they exit. They wave to audience as they leave.*)

Helpers

This is the first of these skits to depend upon a prop: the "crashbox." You don't need a lot of metal utensils to make the desired noise. Again, it is essential that the give-and-take of the actors moves freely and without pause. The final line of the skit can carry a lot of hidden meaning.

Theme

"And let us consider how we may spur one another on toward love and good deeds" (Hebrews 10:24).

Scripture

Matthew 21:28-31

Cast

Actor 1
Actor 2
Actor 3

Props

Large box with pots, pans, and silverware to make noise when dropped.

(Enter Actor 1 *from stage left, carrying box.*)

Actor 1 *(panting hard):* I sure hope I can get this box home. I sure could use some help. I better wait a moment and catch my breath. *(Pants)*

(Enter Actor 2 and Actor 3 *from stage right, talking animatedly to each other.*)

ACTOR 2: . . . and I thought the way the pastor talked about helping people as a way to show them Jesus was great!

ACTOR 3: I have to agree with you. It makes sense that Jesus would want us to help people, since He always helped them.

(ACTOR 2 *and* ACTOR 3 *approach* ACTOR 1 *but don't notice him.*)

ACTOR 2: I feel that I have to carry through on this. *(Bumps into* ACTOR 1) Oh, excuse me. *(To* ACTOR 3) Do you know where I could find someone to help?

ACTOR 3: I've been thinking about that too. Maybe I could go downtown to the Main Street Mission. I can't seem to find anyone to help around here.

ACTOR 1 *(overhearing)*: Uh, excuse me—

ACTOR 2: That's a great idea. It will show everyone at church that we put our beliefs into action.

ACTOR 3: Wait a minute. That's my idea. You go find someone to help. I'm going to get the credit for helping them downtown.

ACTOR 1: Say, gang, I was wondering—

ACTOR 2: Hey! I'm the one who decided to be the big helper around here.

ACTOR 3: Oh, yeah? You couldn't help anyone half as much as I could.

ACTOR 2: Says who??

ACTOR 3: Says me!

ACTOR 1 *(deep breath)*: Do you think one of you could—

ACTOR 2: I'm going to be the best helper!

ACTOR 3: Oh, no, you're not!

ACTOR 2: Oh, yes, I am!

ACTOR 3: Oh, no, you're not!

ACTOR 2: Oh, yes, I am!

ACTOR 1 *(yelling)*: I COULD SURE USE SOME HELP!!

ACTOR 2 and ACTOR 3 *(looking at audience)*: Help?

ACTOR 1: Yeah. I'm trying to get this box home, and it's very heavy—

ACTOR 3 *(moves to* ACTOR 1): Say no more. I am the one to help you. Let's get that box home.

ACTOR 1: Thanks a lot. You're a—

ACTOR 2 *(pushes* ACTOR 3 *aside)*: You need the help of a real helper. And that's me!

(ACTOR 2 *and* ACTOR 3 *move to either side of* ACTOR 1, *who still holds the box.*)

ACTOR 3: Get out of my face! I was here first!

ACTOR 1: Listen, fellas—

ACTOR 2 *(grabs one side of the box)*: Bug off! I'm going to help him!

ACTOR 1: You know you both could—

ACTOR 2 *(to* ACTOR 1*)*: Shut up! I'm helping you.

ACTOR 1: Oh, yeah. I forgot.

ACTOR 3 *(grabs other side of the box)*: No, he isn't. I'm helping you.

ACTOR 1: Maybe I don't need help.

ACTOR 2: Oh, yes, you do. And I'm helping you! *(Pulls box)*

ACTOR 3: I'm the one that's helping him! *(Pulls box)*

(ACTOR 2 *and* ACTOR 3 *start a tug-of-war with the box and* ACTOR 1.)

ACTOR 2: I'm helping!! *(Pulls box)*

ACTOR 3: I'm helping!! *(Pulls box)*

ACTOR 2: I'm helping!! *(Pulls box)*

ACTOR 3: I'm helping!! *(Pulls box)*

ACTOR 2 and ACTOR 3 *(yelling)*: LET GO!!

(*Both pull, but box slips out of their hands and falls. Crash!! All actors look down at the box.* ACTOR 2 *and* ACTOR 3 *look up at audience.*)

ACTOR 2 and ACTOR 3: Ooops.

ACTOR 1: Oh, no.

ACTOR 2: Well . . . uh . . . at least you don't have to carry it home.

ACTOR 3: Or you can carry it home in chunks?

ACTOR 2 *(to* ACTOR 3*)*: Let's get out of here. *(Backing away)* Well, we were sure happy to help.

ACTOR 3 *(also backing away)*: Yeah. Uh . . . anytime, pal. *(Holding up hand)* Don't bother thanking us. Uh . . . God will reward us.

(*Exit* ACTOR 2 *and* ACTOR 3 *quickly.*)

ACTOR 1 *(exits shaking head, looking at box)*: I hope so.

The Invitation

Now we have a skit that could use a larger troupe of players. However, if you do not have a large troupe, three or four people can handle all the parts. This installment of "The Master's Piecemeal Theater" was the one I chose to include in this collection. You may desire to use this format for some of your other skits. Alister Baker Sea should present an aura of dignity and style. The separate scenes should follow on each other closely with no dead time between. Parts may be doubled.

Theme

"And my tongue shall speak of thy righteousness and of thy praise all the day long" (Psalm 35:28, KJV).

Scripture

Acts 18:1-8

Cast

ALISTER BAKER SEA	ACTOR 7
ACTOR 1	ACTOR 8
ACTOR 2	ACTRESS 9
ACTOR 3	VOICE
ACTOR 4	ACTOR 10
ACTOR 5	ACTOR 11
ACTOR 6	

Props

Chair (Living Room Style)
Large Book
Slip of Paper
Bible
Baseball Cap
Menu or Picture of Restaurant

(Enter ALISTER BAKER SEA *with large book.* ALISTER BAKER SEA *should be very cultured; British, if possible. He should calmly take a seat at stage right and open the book.)*

ALISTER: Good evening, ladies and gentlemen. This is Alister Baker Sea, known as A. B. Sea to my friends, with another installment of "The Master's Piecemeal Theater." This week's topic will be that oddity of Christian culture, the Invitation. We hope to observe various methods used by individuals to invite their friends, family, and total strangers to church. Ah, I see we are ready to observe Invitation No. 1.

(Enter ACTOR 1, *very nervous, from stage left, and* ACTOR 2 *from stage right.)*

ALISTER: Our first person. He wants to ask his friend to church and has even rehearsed a speech.

ACTOR 1 *(rehearsing to himself)*: Hi, Ralph. I would like to give you a . . . cordial . . . that's good . . . invitation to attend our church this Sunday. I will be happy . . . no . . . uh . . . delighted to give you a ride. Right, that's good. Oh, oh. Here he comes.

ACTOR 2: Hi, Joe.

ACTOR 1: Uh . . . uh . . . uh . . .

ACTOR 2: What's happening?

ACTOR 1: Uh, Ralph . . . I blah, blea, blo, garble, mumble, aaag, blop, blim.

ACTOR 2 *(startled)*: Uh, right. *(Moves cautiously away)* See you later, Joe. *(Exit* ACTOR 2, *stage left. Exit* ACTOR 1, *stage right, still babbling.)*

ALISTER: I think you noticed that our first person was somewhat fearful. To put it another way, he was scared spitless. This really doesn't happen very often. Usually it is a result of low confidence, self-doubt, or brain damage.

(Enter ACTOR 3 *with slip of paper, from stage left, and* ACTOR 4 *from stage right.)*

ALISTER: Please note that our next person has gone to the trouble of writing out her invitation. This would probably work fine, except for the fact that she cannot read her own handwriting.

ACTOR 4: Hi, Jill. What's happening?

ACTOR 3: Uh . . . Hi, Kathy . . . *(Looking at paper)* . . . I would lick you—

ACTOR 4 *(does a double take)*: Say what??

ACTOR 3 *(looks closer)*: . . . No! no! . . . that's, I would like you to crow with me—

ACTOR 4 *(looks at* ACTOR 3 *and then audience)*: Crow??

ACTOR 3 *(turns paper upside down)*: Oh, sorry, that's come. I would like you to come with me to . . . uh . . . China?? *(Shaking head)* No, that's not it . . . Chino??

ACTOR 4: Look, gal, when you can figure it out, give me a call. *(Exit* ACTOR 4.*)*

ACTOR 3 *(turns and follows* ACTOR 4, *calling after her)*: Church!! That's it!! I would like you to come with me to church!

ALISTER: By george, I think she's got it. There's nothing wrong with planning what you are going to say, but it helps if you can say it.

(Enter ACTOR 5, *with large Bible, from stage left, and* ACTOR 6 *from stage right.)*

ALISTER: Ah, here's an interesting method that I think you'll recognize.

ACTOR 5 *(calling to* ACTOR 6*)*: Hey, you!! Sinner!!

*(*ACTOR 6 *looks around and then at* ACTOR 5.*)*

ACTOR 6 *(points to himself. Word is mouthed, not spoken)*: Me?

ACTOR 5 *(louder)*: Yes, you, sinner!! Come here!

*(*ACTOR 6 *shrugs and comes to center stage, where* ACTOR 5 *meets him.)*

ACTOR 5 *(tightly puts an arm around* ACTOR 6's *shoulder)*: You lost soul. Do you know where you need to be this Sunday?

ACTOR 6 *(tilts head, thinking)*: Well, I guess—

ACTOR 5 *(slaps* ACTOR 6 *on the back, making him choke slightly)*: Don't guess!! Because I know!! The Lord has told me that you, yes, YOU are to be at my church this Sunday!!

ACTOR 6 *(shaking head)*: I don't know; you see—

ACTOR 5 *(grabs* ACTOR 6 *by the arm and shakes him)*: Don't say no to the Lord!!

ACTOR 6: I'm not! How about next week?

ACTOR 5 *(throws* ACTOR 6 *to the ground)*: No!! Next week may be too late!! You must come this Sunday!! *(Shaking* ACTOR 6 *while he is on the ground)* Do you hear me? This Sunday!!

ACTOR 6 (*holding up hands*): OK!! OK!! I'll come!! I'll come!!

ACTOR 5 (*lets go of* ACTOR 6. *Places one foot on him and looks at audience*): Hallelujah! Another lost soul has come home!

(ACTOR 5 *moves foot off* ACTOR 6 *but doesn't look away from audience.* ACTOR 6 *quickly crawls offstage.*)

ACTOR 5: I have invited six people today, and everyone has said yes. (*Turning to where* ACTOR 6 *was*) You will not regret . . . Where did he go? . . . (*Turning back to audience*) That's the sixth one I've lost today too. I don't understand it. (*Looking offstage*) Oh, well, there's someone else. Hey, you!! Sinner!! (*Exit*)

ALISTER: I'm sure you recognized that person as a graduate of the Mike Tyson School of Invitations. Now, here is another interesting method of inviting people to church. It follows the axiom, "If all else fails, bribe them!"

(*Enter* ACTOR 7 *from stage left,* ACTOR 8 *from stage right.*)

ACTOR 7: Hey, Harry! This is your lucky day!

ACTOR 8 (*puzzled*): Oh, hi, George. What do you mean?

ACTOR 7: You get to play "Church of Fortune"!

ACTOR 8: What? I don't understand.

ACTOR 7 (*looking up and out into the audience*): Johnny Goodheart, tell Harry what he might win!

VOICE (*very D.J. voice*): A new hat!!

(ACTOR 8 *looks all around, trying to find the voice. Enter* ACTRESS 9, *à la Vanna White, carrying a cap.*)

VOICE (*very quickly*): This genuine, imitation, leather church cap, with sweatband, washable lining, and our church logo on the front can be yours for simply coming to church this Sunday. (*Exit* ACTRESS 9.)

ACTOR 8 (*embarrassed*): Uh . . . wow . . . uh . . . thanks, George, but I don't really need—

ACTOR 7: But wait!! That's not all! Johnny, tell him what else he could win!

VOICE: A dinner for two!

(*Enter* ACTRESS 9 *carrying a menu or a picture of a restaurant.* ACTOR 8 *sneaks off in the middle of the following description.*)

VOICE: Yes, you and a guest will receive a dinner for two from Pete's Palace of Pork. The dinner includes soup, salad, entrée, and two helpings of Pete's famous pig's foot pie! Yum-yum. All this could be yours if you are at church this Sunday! (*Exit* ACTRESS 9.)

ACTOR 7: Well, what do you say, Harry? Harry?? *(To himself)* I guess we need to make it a dinner for four. *(Exit)*

ALISTER: Yes. This is an oddity of our church culture. The oddity is that many people complicate something that is simple. Watch.

(Enter ACTOR 10 *from stage left and* ACTOR 11 *from stage right.)*

ACTOR 10: Hi, Dave.

ACTOR 11: What's happening, Jim?

ACTOR 10: Quite a bit, Dave. Since you're a friend, I'd like you to know about it.

ACTOR 11: Oh, what's that?

ACTOR 10: Dave, I was wondering if you would like to share something that is very special to me.

ACTOR 11: What do you mean, Jim?

ACTOR 10: Well, my church is really special. We listen, we help, and we care. I'd like you to just come and take a look.

(Exit ACTOR 10 *and* ACTOR 11.*)*

ALISTER: Let's stop right here. Maybe the answer is yes. Maybe it's no. The important thing is the invitation. *(Standing and closing the book)* It really doesn't matter how or where it is made. This is Alister Baker Sea, hoping to see you next week; and—bring a friend.

(Exit)

The Cure

This skit and the two that follow ("Gifts" and "Pharisee . . .") bear some resemblance to the parable of the Good Samaritan. This skit, however, is a metaphor of salvation. The different cures for "soulus voidus" represent how man tries to deal with his inner need, and what we can do to help. This is an example of how comedy can also be convicting.

Theme

"The thief comes only to steal and kill and destroy; I have come that they may have life, and have it to the full" (John 10:10).

Scripture

Luke 10:30-37

Cast

Actor 1
Actor 2
Actor 3
Actor 4
Actor 5

Props

Books and Pamphlets
Two Pill Bottles
Chair

(Enter Actor 1. *When he reaches chair at center stage, he suddenly collapses in the chair, breathing hard.*)

ACTOR 1 *(panting)*: Something's wrong! I'm sick! I feel awful! Help!

(Enter ACTOR 2 *with books and pamphlets.)*

ACTOR 2: What's wrong?

ACTOR 1: I can't catch my breath. I'm dizzy. I feel real hot. And I'm seeing pink dots in front of my eyes. Help me.

ACTOR 2 *(nodding head)*: Yep. I thought so. You've got soulus voidus. That's been going around. *(Pats* ACTOR 1 *on the head)* Don't worry, though, it won't last more than a few hours.

ACTOR 1 *(relieved)*: You mean I'll be OK?

ACTOR 2: No. You'll be dead.

ACTOR 1: What?? Wait a minute!! What can I do?

ACTOR 2: You're in luck! *(Starting to give* ACTOR 1 *books and pamphlets)* I've got loads of literature on soulus voidus. Here, this one tells why you have soulus voidus. This one tells what the symptoms are—

ACTOR 1 *(exasperated)*: I know what the symptoms are! I need help!

ACTOR 2 *(calmly)*: That's what I'm trying to do. This one tells about people who have been cured of soulus voidus. And on the back of this one you'll find our 24-hour hot line phone number that you can call if you have questions. I'm sure that this literature will be of great help. Bye now. *(Exit)*

ACTOR 1 *(still gasping, but overwhelmed, watches* ACTOR 2 *leave)*: I don't believe it. I need help, and he gives me the Library of Congress. *(Tosses literature to the floor)* Help! Anyone!

(Enter ACTOR 3.)

ACTOR 3: Did you cry for help?

ACTOR 1 *(gasping)*: Yes! I'm sick! I've got soulus voidus. I need help to get to the hospital!

ACTOR 3 *(holding up hand)*: Wait. You don't need to go to the hospital to cure yourself of soulus voidus.

ACTOR 1 *(still panting)*: I don't?

ACTOR 3: No. All you need is to draw on that unlimited strength that is flowing throughout the universe.

ACTOR 1: I don't understand.

ACTOR 3: I'll help you. I've done this before with other people who have soulus voidus.

ACTOR 1 *(hopeful)*: Really?? That's great.

ACTOR 3 *(moving behind* ACTOR 1*)*: Now you need to close your eyes and concentrate on your innermost being. *(Places hands on either side of* ACTOR 1's *head and starts rocking back and forth)* Now, become one with the rocks and trees. Draw on their strength. Concentrate. *(Starts to hum)* Ohmmmmm! Ohmmmmmm!

ACTOR 1 *(gasping as he hums)*: Ohmmm! Ohmmm!

ACTOR 3 *(moving away from* ACTOR 1*)*: There you are! You've drawn on the strength of the universe to cure yourself.

ACTOR 1 *(still panting)*: But I still feel sick.

ACTOR 3 *(shaking head)*: Oh, well. We tried.

ACTOR 1 *(frustrated)*: I thought you said you've done this before.

ACTOR 3: I have. *(Shrugging)* But it didn't work then either. *(Hopefully)* But there's always the first time. *(Exit)*

ACTOR 1 *(panting)*: Great! I'm dying, and he goes, "Ohmmmmmm!" Someone!! Help!!

(Enter ACTOR 4 *with bottle of pills.)*

ACTOR 4: What's wrong with you?

ACTOR 1: Please, can you help me get to the hospital? I'm dying of soulus voidus. I need help.

ACTOR 4 *(holding up pills)*: Why go to the hospital when I have the pills to cure soulus voidus right here.

ACTOR 1 *(suspiciously)*: Are you sure?

ACTOR 4 *(takes a pill out)*: Take a look. Aren't they the prettiest little pills you ever saw? They're combinations of the best from hundreds of other pills. Two of these will cure you of anything.

ACTOR 1 *(catching breath)*: Sounds good to me. *(Reaches out for them)*

ACTOR 4 *(pulls away)*: Not so fast. You have to pay for them first.

ACTOR 1: Pay?? I'm dying!!

ACTOR 4 *(shaking head)*: That doesn't matter. No pay, no pill.

ACTOR 1 *(pulls money out of pockets)*: Here! Take all my money! Just give me the pills!

ACTOR 4 *(picks up money)*: Not yet. (ACTOR 1 *does things as* ACTOR 4 *says them.)* Stand up; . . . turn around; . . . jump up and down; . . . roll over; . . . lie dead.

Actor 1 *(lying on the floor, gasping)*: Who's playing?

Actor 4: I guess you've earned them. *(Gives pills to Actor 1)* But if you want water, you have to pat your head and rub your stomach. *(Exit Actor 4.)*

Actor 1 *(still on floor)*: Forget it. All I need is the pills. *(Swallows pills)* Yuck! They taste terrible! *(Starts gasping more)* They're not helping! I'm getting worse! Help! Please! I'm dying!

(Enter Actor 5.)

Actor 5: Oh, no! You've got soulus voidus! *(Helps Actor 1 into chair)*

Actor 1 *(gasping)*: That's right! I don't think there's anything that anyone can do.

Actor 5: Yes, there is. I've got something that will help you.

Actor 1 *(unbelieving)*: Oh, sure. I've heard that before.

Actor 5: No, really! I had soulus voidus too.

Actor 1: You had soulus voidus?

Actor 5: I was cured by these. *(Holds up small bottle)* Here, take one pill and see.

Actor 1 *(still suspicious)*: How much will it cost?

Actor 5: Cost?? Nothing. It's free.

Actor 1 *(taking pill)*: Are you sure this will work?

Actor 5: It did for me.

Actor 1 *(takes the pill and immediately breathes easier)*: It works. *(Stands up)* I feel better.

Actor 5: You're cured. Here. *(Gives bottle to Actor 1)* Take these.

Actor 1 *(looks at bottle)*: Oh, in case I have another attack?

Actor 5 *(shakes head)*: No. One pill is enough to cure you. *(Points to bottle)* That's for you to share with someone else. There are more and more cases of soulus voidus around us each day. It's up to us to spread the cure around.

(Exit Actor 1 and Actor 5.)

The Gifts

This is the only one of my skits included in this collection that was not written to be a comedy. It is an example of storytelling. The actors never say a word and must project their thoughts and emotions through their actions. It's a wonderful change of pace for most drama troupes. The storyteller should be off to the side, trying to focus the audience's attention on the actors.

Theme

"Therefore, I urge you, brothers, in view of God's mercy, to offer your bodies as living sacrifices, holy and pleasing to God—this is your spiritual act of worship" (Romans 12:1).

Scripture

Luke 21:1-4

Cast

STORYTELLER
MAN
OLD BEGGAR
WOUNDED TRAVELER
CRUEL MASTER
SLAVE

Props

Costumes for Cast
A Fine Wool Coat
10 Golden Coins
A Small, but Ornate, Container
Table, Far Stage Right

(Enter STORYTELLER, *who does all the talking in this play.*)

STORYTELLER: Many years ago, in a country far away, a man was called to visit the king of his country.

(*Enter* MAN.)

It was customary for a person called before the king to bring gifts of great worth.

(MAN *gathers together belongings.*)

The man was very poor, but he did have three things that he prized above all others.

(MAN *packs items as* STORYTELLER *relates them.*)

There was a coat made of the warmest wool from the sheep of the high country, 10 ancient gold pieces that had belonged to his grandfather, and a cordial that was said to be able to heal any wound or cure any sickness. With his treasures packed, the man began his journey to visit the king on a cold, crisp day.

(MAN *puts his pack on his back and moves to center stage; at the same time,* OLD BEGGAR *enters from stage left, shivering with cold. The* MAN *sets down his pack. They act out what* STORYTELLER *says.*)

As he traveled down the road, he met an old beggar, shivering with cold. The man paused for a moment. He knew that the beggar could not survive the cold night to come in the rags he now wore. The man looked at the beggar and the fine, woolen coat that he carried as a gift for the king. Surely a king, who would have better coats, would need this simple garment less than a poor beggar who might die without it. So the man gave the beggar the fine, woolen coat.

(*Exit, stage right,* OLD BEGGAR *with coat.* MAN *watches him with smile and picks up his pack as* STORYTELLER *continues. Enter* WOUNDED TRAVELER *from stage left. He silently collapses on floor in front of the* MAN.)

The man turned and continued his journey. But he had not gone far before he came upon a fellow traveler who had been terribly wounded in some terrible accident.

(MAN *puts pack down and kneels beside the* WOUNDED TRAVELER. *Again the actors portray what the* STORYTELLER *says.*)

The man was not a doctor, but he could tell that this person would die soon without care. Unfortunately, the nearest town was miles away, so, without a moment's hesitation, the man used all of the magical cordial to heal the traveler. Amazed, but thankful, the traveler was able to continue on his journey, as was the man with but one gift left.

(MAN *picks up pack and turns as* CRUEL MASTER *and* SLAVE *enter, stage left. Again, they act out* STORYTELLER's *words.*)

> However, the man's adventures were not yet through. As he neared the city where the king lived, he came upon a cruel sight. He beheld a master beating his slave. Now the man hated slavery, and he hated cruelty. So he stepped forward to stop the beating. The cruel master refused to stop, and said there was nothing the man could do. In desperation the man offered to buy the slave. After much bargaining, the price for the slave was agreed to be—just what you would think—10 gold pieces. After paying the cruel master, who left quickly upon receiving his money, the man freed the slave, giving him his pack with its few morsels of food.

(MAN *stares after* SLAVE, *shrugs, and turns toward center stage.*)

> Finally, the man arrived at the castle of the king. He was brought in before his ruler. The question was asked, "What have you brought your king?" After a moment of embarrassed silence, the man said that all he had brought as a gift was himself. "I am yours, Your Majesty," came the sincere statement.

(MAN *bows head, then slowly looks up with amazement.*)

> Imagine the man's surprise when, with a smile, the king said, "What greater gift could I possibly receive than a person who is truly mine." And with great pomp and ceremony, the man was adopted by the king.

(*Exit* MAN.)

> So the man lived in the palace as a prince for the rest of his days, because he had offered the greatest gift he could: himself.

(*Exit all.*)

The Pharisee and Publicity

This story, while similar to the parable of the Good Samaritan, is taken more from the story Jesus told of the Pharisee and publican praying in the Temple. Try to make Morgan look as slick and polished as possible.

Theme

"Whatever you do, work at it with all your heart, as working for the Lord, not for men" (Colossians 3:23).

Scripture

Luke 18:9-14

Cast

MORGAN
P. R.
JESSIE
SAM
REPORTER
OTHER REPORTERS

Props

Make-up Pad
Towel
Money
Pads and Pencils
Cameras, Reporting Gear, etc.

(Enter MORGAN *and P. R. from stage right.)*

MORGAN: Look, P. R., I didn't hire you to tell me I have an image problem. I hired you to take care of the problem.

P. R.: I know, Morgan, but I just wanted to make sure you understood the situation. The voters see you as cold and uncaring.

(Enter JESSIE from stage left.)

MORGAN: OK. How do you propose that we make those idiots vote for me?

JESSIE *(approaching MORGAN and P. R.)*: Excuse me, sir, I was wondering if you could help—

MORGAN *(dismissing JESSIE with a wave of his hand)*: I don't help panhandlers.

JESSIE *(taken aback, but not giving up)*: But I'm not a panhandler. I just need bus fare to get home, then I can pay you—

MORGAN *(viciously)*: Bug off! Can't you see I'm busy?

JESSIE *(shrugs and leaves)*: Sorry to bother you.

MORGAN *(to P. R.)*: If I'm elected, I'm going to put a stop to that. What kind of softhearted fool did he take me for?

P. R. *(snapping fingers with idea)*: That's it! That's how we can solve your image problem!

MORGAN: What are you babbling about?

P. R. *(to JESSIE)*: Hey, you!

JESSIE *(points to himself and moves back toward them)*: Me?

P. R.: Yes, you. How much money do you need?

JESSIE *(excited)*: Only $50.00 for bus fare home. You see my wallet was taken, and—

P. R. *(holding up hand to stop JESSIE)*: Yeah, yeah. Sure. Well, stand right here, and you'll get that money. *(To MORGAN)* It's perfect! Human interest. Poor soul wanting to get home. Bighearted politician gives him bus fare out of the goodness of his heart.

MORGAN: Hmmm. But $50.00 isn't very much. *(To JESSIE)* How about $500?

JESSIE *(shaking head)*: I don't need that much. I'll repay you the $50.00 as soon as I get home. I've got a good job and . . .

P. R. *(to MORGAN)*: Don't worry, Morgan, I'll take care of it in the press release. Now let me go get the media. *(Exit P. R.)*

JESSIE: Excuse me, sir. I hate to rush you, but the bus leaves in 15 minutes. Could I possibly have the money so—

MORGAN *(fiercely)*: Just wait, you ungrateful wretch. You'll get your money in just a minute.

(Enter P. R. with SAM, carrying towel and makeup.)

P. R.: The press will be here soon. Sam, see what you can do.

(SAM puts towel around MORGAN's shoulders and dabs his face with makeup pad.)

SAM: This could take forever. *(Pointing to JESSIE)* What about him?

P. R.: Don't worry about him, he's not important.

JESSIE: Thanks a lot!

P. R. *(to JESSIE)*: Good point! We need you to speak up clearly and loudly when you say thank you for Morgan's gracious gift to you.

JESSIE: Gracious gift?

P. R.: You might mention how no one else would help you, but Morgan has a big heart for those in need.

JESSIE: I think I'm getting sick.

P. R.: Don't be nervous. *(Looks offstage)* Here they come! *(To SAM)* Are you ready, Sam?

SAM *(stepping back and looking at MORGAN)*: As ready as we'll ever be, considering what I have to work with.

MORGAN *(matter-of-factly)*: You're fired.

SAM *(taking towel and makeup. Answers sarcastically)*: Again?

(Enter REPORTER and OTHER REPORTERS from stage right. SAM moves over to other side of JESSIE.)

P. R.: Ladies and gentlemen. We have a brief statement, but first you may take some pictures.

REPORTER: Do we have to?

P. R.: Just do it! *(Moves to JESSIE and SAM)* Could you step back a little? You're in the way.

(While MORGAN puts on a plastic smile and poses for the media, JESSIE and SAM move off to stage left.)

SAM *(dryly)*: Makes you feel real important, doesn't it?

JESSIE *(looks at watch)*: I wish they'd hurry. I need to go.

SAM (*sarcastically*): What? And miss this great media event?

JESSIE: Look. If I didn't need the $50.00 to get home, I wouldn't put up with this.

SAM (*unbelieving*): Fifty dollars?? All you need is $50.00??

JESSIE (*deep breath*): Look. Someone stole my wallet today. All I need is to get home. I've got a good job. I'm not a beggar. (*Exasperated*) This is no big deal! I'll send the money back in today's mail, for crying out loud! (*Pointing to* MORGAN) I didn't want a circus!

P. R. (*looking over to* JESSIE *and* SAM): Shhh! Morgan is going to make a statement. (*Hands sheet of paper to* MORGAN.)

(*While* MORGAN *is making his statement to the press,* SAM *reaches into his pocket and gives* JESSIE *some bills.* JESSIE *gives* SAM *a pad of paper and a pencil.* SAM *writes down his name and address and returns the pad and pencil to* JESSIE. JESSIE *and* SAM *shake hands.* SAM *exits stage left.* JESSIE *puts away pad, pencil, and money and starts to leave.*)

MORGAN (*sickly sweet*): Ladies and gentlemen. Today while walking the streets of our fair city, I noticed a poor, destitute individual. My heart went out to this lost soul. I approached him and inquired how I could help him. While I do not seek publicity for this act of kindness, we can hope that it will show my constituents that I have a human side too. . . . (*Notices* JESSIE *leaving*) Wait a minute! (*Turns to P. R., speaks harshly*) P. R., where is that fool going? We're not done yet! (*Turns back to media with plastic smile*)

P. R. (*runs and grabs* JESSIE's *arm. Stage whisper*): What are you doing?? We're in the middle of this event. Don't you want the money?

(REPORTERS *start to move toward* P. R. *and* JESSIE.)

JESSIE (*removing* P. R.'s *hand*): As a matter of fact, no.

REPORTER (*moving closer*): Do I understand you don't want Morgan to help you?

JESSIE: He's not helping me. He's helping himself. I don't need his help. Someone who really cares has helped me, and he didn't do it for everyone to see. Now, if you'll excuse me. I have a bus to catch. (*Exit stage left*)

(REPORTERS *start to exit stage right, writing in note pads as they leave.*)

P. R. (*following* REPORTERS): I'm sorry that you folks didn't get a story.

REPORTER: Oh, we got a story all right. "Candidate Makes Fool of Self in Publicity Stunt!" It will make great reading.

(*Exit* REPORTERS, *leaving* MORGAN *with his plastic smile and* P. R. *staring after them.*)

P. R. *(slowly turning to* MORGAN*)*: Well, Morgan, I think I can truthfully say that you no longer have an image problem.

MORGAN *(astonished)*: Really?

P. R. *(nodding)*: Yes. I think we can now call it an image crisis.

(Exit MORGAN *and* P. R. *stage right.)*

Where Angels Fear to Tread

Knowing that I have been a parent, a school administrator, a schoolteacher, and more precisely, a kindergarten teacher over the past several years, I think you can understand where I received my inspiration for Rhoda. It has always amused me that Peter should make it through so many hardships and barriers, only to be stopped by a girl at the front door of the house. Make Rhoda as brassy, but cute, as you can. Remember, Peter was a big, strong fisherman, reduced to begging by this little girl.

Theme

"Let those who love the Lord hate evil, for he guards the lives of his faithful ones and delivers them from the hand of the wicked" (Psalm 97:10).

Scripture

Romans 12:1-16

Cast

PETER
RHODA

Props

Door

INTRODUCTION *(optional):* God had brought Peter through chains, locks, guards, and dungeons. But Peter still had to overcome the greatest barrier known to man: children!!

(Door center stage. Enter PETER *from stage right.)*

PETER: I can't believe it! It's a miracle! God sent an angel to deliver me from prison. Wait until the church hears about this. Everyone must be worried sick about me.

(PETER *knocks on door. Enter* RHODA *from stage left.*)

RHODA *(melodically)*: Who is it?

PETER *(dramatically)*: It is I! Peter!

RHODA *(pause)*: Peter who??

PETER *(taken aback)*: Uh . . . Peter. Simon Peter. Don't you know me?

RHODA: No-o-o, and Mommy told me, "Never talk to strangers."

PETER: Oh. What's your name, little girl?

RHODA: My name is Rhoda, and I'm not a little girl. I'm . . . *(holds up hand)* five years old.

PETER: I'm pleased to meet you, Rhoda. Now, open the door.

RHODA: No-o-o. Mommy says, "Never talk to strangers."

PETER: Rhoda, I'm not a stranger. I know John Mark, his mother, Mary, and his Uncle Barnabas. This is their house, right?

RHODA: Ye-e-es. Do you know me?

PETER: No, but—

RHODA: My mommy says . . .

PETER and RHODA: "Never talk to strangers."

PETER: Rhoda, listen, it's getting cold out here. *(As* PETER *talks,* RHODA *begins to play finger games and hum to herself.)* I'm tired and hungry, and it's been a long day, so please, go get your mommy, or someone else, to open this door, OK? *(Pause)* OK??

RHODA *(not really listening)*: OK. *(Continues to play and hum)*

PETER: It will be the biggest miracle of the night if I get through this door. *(Getting suspicious)* It's been an awfully long time. *(Listens closely at door, then knocks)* Rhoda??

RHODA: Huh?

PETER: Did you do it?

RHODA: Do what?

PETER *(rubbing forehead)*: Rhoda, will you please go tell the grown-ups that I'm at the front door?

RHODA: No-o-o. Mommy says never interrupt them when they're praying. *(Folds hands as if praying)* And they're praying right now for somebody named Simon.

PETER: Rhoda! That's me! Simon Peter! Please, look through the little window at me. Maybe you'll recognize me.

(RHODA *looks through a window in the door.* PETER *smiles a big smile.*)

RHODA *(making a face)*: Oooo! You look aww-ful!

PETER *(patiently)*: I know, Rhoda. King Herod put me into prison.

RHODA: Why?

PETER *(sigh)*: Because I was preaching that Jesus died for us—

RHODA: Why?

PETER *(deep breath)*: Because He loves us. Now—

RHODA: Why?

PETER *(through gritted teeth)*: I don't know! Now look, Rhoda, let's make it simple. Find any grown-up and just tell them, "Peter is at the door." Can you say that?

RHODA: Peter is at the door.

PETER *(sweetly)*: I knew you could. Now, let's try it again.

(RHODA *repeats it.* PETER *and* RHODA *say it together a few times, until* RHODA *exits singing it over and over.* PETER *is also quietly singing it to himself.*)

PETER *(stopping himself)*: Good grief! I'm starting to sound like her! I wonder if talking to children can give you brain damage?

(*Enter* RHODA *still singing, "Peter is at the door."*)

PETER: Rhoda! Did you tell them?

RHODA: Ye-e-es!

PETER: Are they coming to open the door?

RHODA: No-o-o!

PETER *(frustrated)*: Why not?

RHODA: They said that you can't be Peter. Mommy said you must be Peter's ghost. *(Pause)* Mister, are you a ghost?

PETER: No! I'm not a ghost—yet!

RHODA: Then you can't be Peter.

PETER: But I am Peter!! *(To himself)* I think . . . at least . . . I was when I got here. *(Pats chest)* Yeah, I'm Peter.

RHODA: Then, if you're Peter, you must be a ghost.

PETER: If you say so. *(To himself)* Anything to get inside. *(To RHODA)* All right. I'm Peter, and I'm a ghost. Now will you please open the door!

RHODA: No-o-o. If you're a ghost, you don't need me to open the door, because you can float right through it.

PETER *(pauses. To audience)*: The scary thing is, she's beginning to make sense. *(To RHODA)* Rhoda, are you still there?

RHODA: Yes, Mr. Ghost.

PETER: Look, Rhoda. *(Starts calmly but builds in intensity and volume)* I am Peter. All those people are praying for me, and God has answered their prayers. I need to tell them about it! So please, Rhoda, if you won't open the door, will you just unlock it??

RHODA: No-o-o.

PETER *(losing control)*: WHY NOT!!

RHODA *(pause)*: Because it's not locked.

(PETER pauses, looks at audience and up at heaven. Slowly PETER opens the door and steps through.)

PETER *(keeping control with great effort)*: Why didn't you tell me?

RHODA *(innocently)*: You didn't ask. And Mommy says . . .

PETER and RHODA: "Never talk to strangers."

PETER: Come, Rhoda. Let's go talk to Mommy.

(Exit PETER and RHODA.)

Blind Bart

Not everyone is happy when Jesus comes and changes lives. It can cramp their style. Abigail in this story enjoys being able to complain and boss her blind brother around. Bart is meek and puts up with it until Jesus comes. Then he becomes bold when he realizes a miracle is within his grasp. The disciples should show very little emotion until they try to prevent Bart from being noticed by Jesus.

Theme

"Rejoice with those who rejoice; mourn with those who mourn" (Romans 12:15).

Scripture

Mark 10:46-52; Luke 15:25-32

Cast

ABIGAIL
BART
DISCIPLE 1
DISCIPLE 2
VOICE OFFSTAGE
VOICE OF JESUS OFFSTAGE

Props

Chair
Sunglasses for Bart and Disciples
Suit Coats and Ties for Disciples
Megaphone
Cane for Bart

(Enter BART, *with cane and wearing sunglasses, led by* ABIGAIL.)

ABIGAIL *(frustrated)*: I don't know why I always have to be the one stuck with leading you around.

BART: I'm sorry, Abigail. I hate to be a bother.

ABIGAIL: Don't give me that! You love the attention. I don't see why you can't bring yourself out here to the city wall.

BART: Jericho is a big city. Now, if I had a dog to lead me, Abby—

ABIGAIL *(upset)*: Don't call me Abby!! I hate it!! And don't start in about the Seeing Eye dog again. You know I hate dogs. If you need an animal to lead you around, why don't you use George?

BART: Thanks, but no thanks, Abigail. I don't think George would do very well. I've never heard of a seeing-eye turtle.

ABIGAIL: That's right. I give a constructive suggestion, and you shoot it down. *(They arrive at the chair.)* Well, here we are at your chair.

BART *(touching chair with cane)*: Thank you, Abigail. *(Turns to sit down)*

ABIGAIL *(looking closely at chair)*: Why, this chair is filthy!

(ABIGAIL *pulls the chair out from under* BART *just as he is about to sit, causing him to fall to the ground.* ABIGAIL *brushes the chair off.*)

ABIGAIL *(looking down at* BART*)*: Will you get up off the ground! You are making a fool of yourself and me!

BART *(sighs and stands)*: Sorry, Abigail.

ABIGAIL *(puts chair down and pushes* BART *down into it)*: Now sit down and be quiet!

BART *(sigh)*: Yes, Abigail.

(Enter DISCIPLES *dressed like Secret Service agents.* DISCIPLE 2 *carries a megaphone, concealed from the audience as well as possible.*)

DISCIPLE 1 *(to* DISCIPLE 2*)*: Well, here we are at the North Gate. You better check in with the others. Use the walkie-talkie.

DISCIPLE 2: Roger. *(Pulls out megaphone. Shouts through it to back of building)* Advance team to base!! Have reached objective!! Will reconnoiter the perimeter and advise you on security status!! Over!!

VOICE 1 *(offstage)*: Roger!! Check in when security sweep is complete!! Base clear!!

DISCIPLE 2: Advance team clear!! *(Puts megaphone down)*

BART *(tilting his head to hear better)*: What's going on, Abby?

ABIGAIL *(punches* BART *in shoulder):* Don't call me Abby!! *(Looks at* DISCIPLES*)* I think someone special is going to come by soon. Maybe I should offer my help.

BART *(sarcastically):* I'm sure they'll appreciate your help as much as I do.

(DISCIPLES *approach* ABIGAIL *and* BART.)

ABIGAIL: Here they come. I'll just find out who is coming and give them a little advice.

BART *(sighing):* May God have mercy on their souls.

DISCIPLE 1 *(pointing up):* Do you think we can expect any trouble from anyone in those sycamore trees?

DISCIPLE 2 *(nodding):* We better check them out. Remember what happened the last time He came into Jericho.

ABIGAIL: Could I help you? I live here in Jericho. Maybe I could answer some questions or give some advice?

DISCIPLE 1: Thank you, ma'am. But we just need to check to see if everything is secure for Jesus' arrival this morning.

ABIGAIL: Jesus?

BART *(swinging head toward* DISCIPLES): Jesus?? Did you say, Jesus??

DISCIPLE 2: Who is that?

ABIGAIL: Oh, that's just my blind brother, Bart. He's a pain to me but harmless to everyone else. *(To* BART*)* Shhh!

BART: But don't you understand, Abigail? Jesus is coming! They say He is the Messiah! That means He could heal me!

DISCIPLE 1: Oh, great! Another sickie. I hoped for once we could avoid them.

ABIGAIL *(to* BART): Now Bart, you keep quiet. You're just making things more difficult for these people.

DISCIPLE 1 *(to* DISCIPLE 2): What do you think we should do?

ABIGAIL: Don't concern yourselves about Bart. I can control him.

DISCIPLE 2 *(looking around):* Well, he is the only one around. And the rest of the group is waiting to come into town. *(To* ABIGAIL) Are you sure you can keep him quiet?

ABIGAIL: I assure you, Bart won't say a word.

BART *(standing up):* But Abby, it's Jesus!!

ABIGAIL *(pushing* BART *back down into the chair)*: Don't call me Abby!! Now, sit down and shut up!! I don't want to hear another word from you!!

BART *(sighing)*: Yes, Abigail.

DISCIPLE 1: Everything else looks OK. Why don't you call in?

DISCIPLE 2: Roger. *(Taking megaphone again)* Base, this is advance team!! Security sweep completed!! All clear!! Over!!

VOICE 1 *(offstage)*: We copy, advance team!! We're coming in!! Base clear!!

DISCIPLE 2 *(to everyone)*: They're on their way.

BART *(to himself)*: I know Jesus could heal me.

ABIGAIL *(kicking chair or hitting* BART): Shhh! You've been enough trouble for one day.

DISCIPLE 1 *(pointing off to right)*: There they are!

ABIGAIL *(looking that direction)*: So that's Jesus.

BART *(suddenly standing, waving arms and yelling)*: Jesus! Son of David! Have mercy on me!

(DISCIPLES *look around, trying to think of what to do.*)

ABIGAIL *(horrified, tries to force* BART *to sit down)*: Bart!! Sit down and shut up!! You're making a fool of yourself and embarrassing me!

BART: No way, Sister. This is my only chance! *(Yells again)* Jesus! Son of David! Have mercy on me!

(ABIGAIL *places her hand over* BART's *mouth and tries to force him to sit.* DISCIPLES *stand in front of* BART *to screen him from Jesus.*)

VOICE OF JESUS: Stop!

(*All movement stops.* DISCIPLES *move from* BART *slowly.*)

VOICE OF JESUS: What do you want of Me?

BART: Jesus, I know You can take the darkness away and heal my eyes. Please, Jesus, let me see.

VOICE OF JESUS: Let it be as you say. You are healed.

(DISCIPLES *exit stage left.* BART *removes his dark glasses and begins to look around.* ABIGAIL *just stares at him, disgusted.*)

BART: I can see!! And look, everything is beautiful!! I can see the sky!! It's beautiful!! I can see that bird!! It's beautiful!! I can see that tree!! It's beautiful!! *(Turning to face* ABIGAIL) I can see my sister!! . . . *(Pause. Turns away.)* . . . I can see that flower!! It's beautiful!!

ABIGAIL: Well, you really made a spectacle of yourself this time. I hope you're satisfied.

BART *(shaking head):* Not yet. I've just started. I know there are other things I can see if I follow Jesus. I'm going to find Him. *(Gets a mischievous smile)* See you later—Abby! *(Runs offstage)* I can see!

ABIGAIL *(picking up chair and following):* I'll help you see stars, Bart! *(To audience)* I liked him better blind. *(Exit)*

Behold and Beware

Christmas is a happy time, and this is one of my happiest skits. This has been my kids' favorite skit right from its beginning. The kids, in fact, have caused me to rewrite it often, by placing their personalities into the roles with such abandon. Do the same. Use it as a framework, and let your group change it to fit their personalities.

Theme

"For God so loved the world that he gave his one and only Son, that whoever believes in him shall not perish but have eternal life" (John 3:16).

Scripture

Luke 2:8-16

Cast

SHEPHERD 1 (Pessimistic; Grouchy; Doubting)
SHEPHERD 2 (Optimistic; Calming; "Mary Poppins")
SHEPHERD 3 (Resident Space Cadet; Airhead à la Valley Girl)
ANGEL (It's been a rough day; Counterpart of SHEPHERD 1)

Props

Shepherd's Staff
Flashlight
Costumes (If possible, have the shepherds dress in traditional costumes with the angel dressed in white with wings. SHEPHERD 3 should look a little strange, i.e., sunglasses, tennis shoes, Walkman earphones, etc.)

(Enter SHEPHERDS *from stage left.* SHEPHERD 1 *has staff.*)

SHEPHERD 1: What a day I've been having! All this trouble over three measly little sheep!

SHEPHERD 2: You know every sheep is important!

SHEPHERD 3: Like . . . uh . . . yeah! I think . . . like . . . uh . . . we should be happy about finding lost sheepies.

SHEPHERD 1: Sure, no thanks to you.

SHEPHERD 2: Now, now, relax. He truthfully thought that shape in the shadows was a sheep. Besides, nobody made you jump on it.

SHEPHERD 1 *(glares at* SHEPHERD 3*)*: How could anyone mistake a cactus for a sheep??

SHEPHERD 3: Like, it looked furry. And like, I still think we should be happy about finding the lost sheepies.

SHEPHERD 1 *(builds in anger)*: Happy!! You want happy!! OK, I'm happy!! Why shouldn't I be happy? Here we are, stumbling around in the cold and dark while our friends are gathered around a nice, warm campfire. Look! *(Motions off to stage right)* We're still miles away, and you can see the glow from here!! They're even having a party without us!! HAPPY?? *(Screams)* I'M HAPPY!!!

SHEPHERD 3: Like, that's better.

(SHEPHERD 1 *starts to swing staff to hit* SHEPHERD 3, *but* SHEPHERD 2 *stops him. Enter* ANGEL *from stage right, carrying flashlight in left hand.)*

ANGEL: What a day I've been having! All this trouble over three measly little shepherds. *(Sees* SHEPHERDS*)* Ah! There they are, finally. I guess I had better give them the traditional angel greeting. *(Clears throat; straightens back)* Yo! Hey, you!!

SHEPHERD 2: Who is that?

SHEPHERD 3: Like, it looks like a big, white birdie.

ANGEL *(looks up to heaven)*: Why me? I could have been working with the star, You know. *(Turning back to the* SHEPHERDS; *talks with great pomp)* I am the Angel of the Lord. Do not be afraid.

SHEPHERD 2 *(shrugging)*: We're not. *(To* SHEPHERD 1*)* Are you afraid?

SHEPHERD 1 *(shaking head)*: I'm not afraid. *(To* SHEPHERD 3*)* Are you afraid?

SHEPHERD 3 *(puzzled)*: Like, why should I be afraid of a big, white birdie?

ANGEL *(hurt)*: Well, I thought I'd get at least . . . you know . . . a little scream or something.

(SHEPHERD 1 *looks at* SHEPHERD 2, *who looks at* SHEPHERD 3. *All* SHEPHERDS *look back at* ANGEL.)

SHEPHERD 3: Like . . .

SHEPHERDS *(halfhearted)*: Aah.

ANGEL *(near tears)*: Don't patronize me! That only makes it worse! *(Puts hand to forehead)*

SHEPHERD 2 *(cheerfully)*: I know. When angels come, the glory of the Lord is supposed to shine round about us. How about shining a little glory for us?

(SHEPHERD 3 *jumps up and down, clapping hands.*)

ANGEL *(shaking head)*: I don't think so.

SHEPHERD 1 *(demanding)*: Come on! Give us a little glory!

ANGEL *(sarcastically)*: Glory? You want glory? Fine! You've got it. Glory!! (ANGEL *points flashlight at* SHEPHERDS *and turns it on.*) Behold.

SHEPHERD 2: This really hasn't been a good day for you, has it?

SHEPHERD 3 *(raising hand)*: Like, I think you need, you know, new batteries.

ANGEL: Can I just say my piece and leave?

SHEPHERD 2 *(brightly)*: I have an idea.

SHEPHERD 1: Oh, no.

SHEPHERD 2: They say angel music is beautiful. Why don't you sing us your message? That will cheer everybody up!

(SHEPHERD 3 *jumps up and down, clapping hands.*)

ANGEL: I don't know . . .

SHEPHERD 2: Sure. That will help. *(To other* SHEPHERDS, *nodding head)* We want to hear him, don't we?

SHEPHERD 1: No.

SHEPHERD 3: Yeah! *(To* ANGEL*)* Like, do you know "Twinkle, Twinkle, Little Star"?

(SHEPHERD 2 *smiles at* ANGEL *and stomps on* SHEPHERD 3's *foot.* SHEPHERD 3 *stands still for a moment and reacts slowly, holding foot and silently saying, "Like, ow."*)

SHEPHERD 2: I just know that when you sing your message of joy to us in that beautiful angel music, we'll all feel great!

ANGEL *(doubtfully)*: Well, OK. *(Clears throat and hums to set pitch.* ANGEL *begins to sing—offpitch.)* "Noel, Noel, Noel, Noel, Born is the King of Israel."

SHEPHERD 1 *(pauses; very sarcastically)*: Oh, I feel much better.

SHEPHERD 3: Now can you sing "Twinkle, Twinkle, Little Star"?

SHEPHERD 2: Wait a minute. What was that about a King being born?

ANGEL *(very little enthusiasm)*: Over in Bethlehem, in a stable, Messiah has been born.

SHEPHERD 2 *(excited)*: Messiah has come!

(SHEPHERD 3 *jumps up and down and claps hands.*)

SHEPHERD 1: Hold your camels there. Why would Messiah be born in a stable in a little town like Bethlehem? There's nothing special there.

SHEPHERD 3: Like . . . uh . . . maybe Messiah isn't supposed to be special.

SHEPHERD 1: What??

SHEPHERD 2: Wait! He may have a point. If Messiah is supposed to understand our troubles and pain, He probably would be born to a poor and humble family. *(Pointing to* SHEPHERD 3, *who is spaced out)* He may be right!

SHEPHERD 1 *(staring at* SHEPHERD 3*)*: That's frightening.

ANGEL: Well, if that's settled, I'll be going.

SHEPHERD 1: Not so fast. There are more important people around here, you know. Why are you telling us instead of them?

ANGEL *(exasperated)*: How am I supposed to know!? I give messages, not answers.

SHEPHERD 2: I know. Messiah is coming to help the people in need. He will belong to all of us, not just the wealthy or powerful.

SHEPHERD 1 *(to* SHEPHERD 3*)*: What do you think, King Solomon?

SHEPHERD 3 *(waking from daydream)*: Huh?? Oh . . . like, it works for me.

ANGEL: Great. Now why don't you folks run on down to Bethlehem and find your Messiah?

SHEPHERD 1: How will we know that we've found Him?

ANGEL: Look. It's the only stable with a newborn baby lying in a manger. You can't miss it. Besides, there's this big star shining right over it. Any idiot—

SHEPHERD 3 *(starts singing)*: "Twinkle, twinkle, little star . . ." *(Continues humming)*

ANGEL *(pointing to* SHEPHERD 3*)*: Maybe you should just put a leash on him and lead him there.

SHEPHERD 2: Fantastic!! Let's go!

(SHEPHERDS *start to exit, leading* SHEPHERD 3 *by the hand.*)

SHEPHERD 1 *(stopping)*: I almost forgot. *(Runs back to* ANGEL. *Hands staff to him.)* Somebody's got to watch the sheep. *(Pats* ANGEL *on the shoulder)* Thanks for the good news. *(Waving)* Bye!

(SHEPHERDS *exit, with* SHEPHERD 3 *still humming and waving to anyone.*)

ANGEL *(calling after* SHEPHERDS): Wait a minute!! I don't even like sheep! Like, what a day I've been having. *(Exit* ANGEL.)

A Funny Thing Happened . . .

Until recently, I couldn't think of a comedic theme that fit Easter. Then it hit me: Mankind had done everything it could to beat Jesus, and it lost—badly! Someone had to be the first to break the news to the losers. That person probably had a tough time doing it. Antonius should put a lot of body language into his part to show how uncomfortable he is with his message.

Theme

"By his power God raised the Lord from the dead, and he will raise us also" (1 Corinthians 6:14).

Scripture

Matthew 28:1-15

Cast

PILATE
ANTONIUS

Props

Small Table
Pitcher
Two Goblets
Roman Costumes (if possible)

INTRODUCTION *(optional):* At Easter we have the joy of the empty tomb. We remember how the women and the disciples rejoiced at Jesus' resurrection. And this is as it should be. But have you ever thought how the soldiers at the tomb had to break the news to their superiors about Easter morning?

(Enter PILATE to stand at table in center stage. Enter ANTONIUS cautiously.)

PILATE: Ah, Antonius. Come in, come in. Have some wine.

ANTONIUS *(holding up hand)*: Thank you, Governor, sir. But I need to talk to you, sir.

PILATE *(taking his own goblet)*: Ah, yes. I'm sure you want to talk about your duties over the past few days. It must seem strange.

ANTONIUS *(deep breath)*: Strange would hardly describe what happened this morning, sir.

PILATE *(not listening)*: You want to know why I would put my best centurion in charge of a simple execution and the guarding of a tomb. I don't imagine that it was very exciting.

ANTONIUS: As a matter of fact, sir, it had its moments. . . .

PILATE: Well, it was a ticklish business, Antonius. And I knew you could handle it. I told my wife, "If Antonius can't handle this, I'm a Nubian parrot."

ANTONIUS: That does paint an interesting picture, sir. But, you see—

PILATE: And you did a great job handling the crowd during that darkness on Friday. Wasn't that the scariest thing you ever saw?

ANTONIUS: Wel-l-l-l, actually, this morning—

PILATE: Then all those people start talking about this Jesus being the Son of God. But I knew you wouldn't fall for that, would you, Antonius?

(ANTONIUS nods his head very quickly. But PILATE has turned away.)

PILATE: In fact, I told the tribune, "Don't worry, Claudius, if Antonius can't take care of things, I'm a Nubian parrot."

ANTONIUS: You're too kind, sir. But I need to tell you about the tomb. You see—

PILATE: Of course, the tomb. I bet that big stone didn't move too easily. But once in place, the gods themselves couldn't move it.

ANTONIUS: It's funny you should mention that, sir—

PILATE: I never did really check it. You did put my seal on it.

ANTONIUS: Oh, yes sir, but—

PILATE: I knew it. I told Herod, "Antonius will take care of the guard, or I'm a Nubian parrot."

ANTONIUS: I really wish you would stop saying that, sir.

PILATE *(smiling)*: Isn't that just like a Roman soldier. You can't take a compliment, but you have the courage to stand up to the devil himself.

ANTONIUS: The devil, yes. However, what we saw today—

PILATE: Oh, did you see anyone important around the tomb this morning?

ANTONIUS (*shrugging*): Uh . . . yeah . . . I . . . I guess you could say that.

PILATE: Joseph of Arimathea, right? That man is a pain! He pestered me for two hours about getting that body from the Cross. I think he would have been happier if he could have taken it to his house!

ANTONIUS: It might have saved some trouble, sir—

PILATE: I just don't understand him. Now he has a new tomb that he paid for, but he'll never be able to use it.

ANTONIUS: Oh, I don't know about that.

PILATE: And those women. I'll bet they were your biggest problem.

ANTONIUS: Nooo. I don't think so.

PILATE: Ah, noble Antonius. Always kind to the ladies. (*Sternly*) You didn't move the stone for them, did you?

ANTONIUS: I can truthfully say we didn't touch the stone.

PILATE: Good. I don't care if they want to embalm the body or not. No man is to open that tomb!

ANTONIUS: I can promise you that, sir, but you see—

PILATE: Good man. I remember telling that rat Caiaphas, "Antonius will take care of the tomb, or I'm a Nubian parrot."

ANTONIUS: Sir, there's nothing to take care of.

PILATE: I understand, Antonius. . . .

ANTONIUS: I don't think you do, sir. . . .

PILATE: Of course I do. You're thinking, Why guard this tomb? A dead body isn't going to just walk away!

ANTONIUS: Believe me, sir, that's not what I'm thinking now!

PILATE: Well, you see, this Jesus claimed that He would rise from the dead in three days. So you see, we had to keep a guard until today. As if there was anything to worry about, right? I mean, if Jesus could rise again, I'm a Nubian parrot.

ANTONIUS: Well, sir—

PILATE: Come on, what do you say to that, Antonius? (*Smiling*) Am I right, or am I a Nubian parrot?

ANTONIUS: Polly want a cracker??

PILATE: What??

ANTONIUS: As a matter of fact, we did have a slight problem today.

PILATE: What do you mean by "slight problem"?

ANTONIUS *(deep breath and said quickly):* There was the earthquake, the angel, the stone rolling away, and Jesus saying, "Good morning, Palestine."

PILATE: You mean Jesus is alive??

ANTONIUS: As alive as I am, sir.

PILATE *(grimly):* I think we can fix that.

ANTONIUS *(swallowing hard):* I think I'll take that drink now, sir.

PILATE: Never mind that! We need to get a story out to the people. How about saying that His disciples stole the body?

ANTONIUS: But I told you the truth, sir—

PILATE: Truth! I don't want the truth! I want a story that keeps us out of trouble!

ANTONIUS *(stiffly):* Sir, I cannot lie! I have my honor as a Roman soldier.

PILATE: Of course, Antonius, of course. You have a choice. You can tell the truth . . . and lose your head; or you can forget your honor, help me with the story, and be transferred to Britain. The choice is yours. *(Exit)*

ANTONIUS *(pause; then in British accent):* I say, ol' chap. What are the fashions like in London these days? Pip-pip. Cheerio. *(Exit)*

You Were There

Here it is! If you're tired of little 5-minute skits, here is a 20-minute comedy-playlet. It uses puns, sarcasm, slapstick, and any other mode of comedy I could think of. It has been a big hit whenever I've performed it. It takes a lot of work, but it sure is fun.

Theme

"By faith Noah, when warned about things not yet seen, in holy fear built an ark to save his family. By his faith he condemned the world and became heir of the righteousness that comes by faith" (Hebrews 11:7).

Scripture

Genesis 6; 7; 8

Cast

WALTER CRANKCASE	NOAH	SHEM
HAM	JAPHETH	MRS. NOAH
HECKLER 1	HECKLER 2	SIGN PERSON

Props

Telephone	Scuba Mask	Storm Noises
Sign, "TIME"	Mountain	Sign, "Mount Ararat"
Hair Dryer	Long Board	Shoe Box
Large Branch	Sailing Clothes	Scrolls
Map	Theme Music	Sign, "The End"
Hammer and Sawing Noises		

(Music begins and WALTER CRANKCASE *enters. Music fades.)*

WALTER: Welcome, ladies and gentlemen, boys and girls, to "You Were There." I'm your host, Walter Crankcase. Today we would like to take you back and meet that great boatbuilder, Noah! So with the magic of imagination, let's begin our visit to the shop of Noah and Sons.

(Music begins. Enter NOAH with phone. Music fades.)

NOAH *(speaking on phone)*: Uh . . . right. Let's see if I've got this right: 300 cubits long, 50 cubits wide, and 30 cubits high, right? And what type of wood was that? Gopher wood. Right.

WALTER: Excuse me, Noah, I wonder if we could talk to you for a moment?

NOAH: Sure. Just a second, this is kind of important.

WALTER: Well, we've come quite a long way to see you. Who is that anyway?

NOAH: God.

WALTER: Feel free to finish your call.

NOAH: Thank you. *(Speaking into phone)* Now, about the animals . . . two by two . . . plus enough for food. We'll get to work right away. Good-bye.

WALTER: Wow! You were actually talking to God!

NOAH: Yep! But anybody can talk with Him. It's just that not many people try.

WALTER: So you just now got the instructions about building the ark?

NOAH: That's right. Well, can't stand around here talking. Got to get to work. *(Exit NOAH.)*

WALTER *(to audience)*: I guess if we're going to find out more about this story, we're going to have to stay around for a while. You see, right after Noah was told how big to build the ark, he started, but it took Noah many years to finish.

(Sounds of hammering and sawing start.)

WALTER: Time passes.

(PERSON carrying sign "TIME" passes across the stage. Enter NOAH.)

WALTER: Well, Noah, how is the big boat coming?

NOAH: Not bad. We're right on schedule.

WALTER: What is the ark going to look like?

NOAH: Well, it's going to be of the most modern design. Every line will be clean and beautiful. It's going to be the fanciest ship afloat.

WALTER: Sounds impressive. Do you have a model of the modern, beautiful, fancy ship?

NOAH: Sure do. *(Holds up shoe box)* There it is. Isn't she a beauty?

WALTER: That's going to be the fanciest, most modern, most beautiful ship afloat?

NOAH: Yep, and the only ship afloat.

WALTER: I see. Who's helping you build the ark?

NOAH: My sons: Shem, Japheth, and Ham.

WALTER: Could we talk to them for a moment?

NOAH: Sure. Good luck. *(Exit NOAH.)*

WALTER *(yelling offstage):* Shem! Ham! Japheth! Could you come here a second?

(Enter SHEM, JAPHETH, and HAM, with board over shoulder.)

SHEM: Sure thing. The name's Shem. *(Shakes hands with WALTER CRANKCASE)*

JAPHETH: I'm Japheth. *(Shakes hands with WALTER CRANKCASE)*

WALTER *(to HAM):* So you must be Ham.

HAM: Duh . . . that's right! I think. *(Moves to stand between SHEM and JAPHETH, facing audience)*

WALTER: Could I ask you boys some questions?

HAM: Sure.

(HAM swings toward WALTER, barely missing SHEM with the board, who ducks.)

SHEM: Hey! Watch what you're doing, dummy!

HAM: Sorry, Shem.

(HAM swings toward SHEM, barely missing JAPHETH with the board, who ducks.)

JAPHETH: You almost did it again, Ham. Watch what you're doing!

HAM: I'm trying.

(HAM swings toward JAPHETH, hitting SHEM with the board with a loud whack. SHEM should stumble or crawl off the stage, holding his head.)

JAPHETH: Shem!

HAM: Where?

(HAM swings around, hitting JAPHETH with the board with a loud whack. JAPHETH should stumble or crawl off the stage holding his head.)

HAM: I can't see him, Japheth. Japheth? Japheth? I wonder where they went. *(Moves closer to WALTER CRANKCASE)*

WALTER: I think they got a little bored and left. *(To audience)* Get it? A little board? *(Dismisses audience)* Ah, forget it.

HAM: They're always leaving me alone.

(HAM *swings around, hitting* WALTER *with the board with a loud whack.* WALTER *now should stumble for a moment.*)

WALTER *(holding head):* I think I know why.

(HAM *swings around, barely missing* WALTER *with the board, who ducks.*)

HAM: Well, why don't you ask me some questions?

WALTER: Why not? I'm already numb. How is the work on the boat going, Ham?

HAM: Real good, Mr. Crankcase. We are right on schedule. We'd be ahead of schedule, but we keep having so many accidents.

WALTER: I think I know why.

NOAH *(from offstage):* Ham! Bring me that board.

(HAM *swings around, hitting* WALTER *with the board with a loud whack.* WALTER *should stumble or crawl off the stage, holding his head.*)

HAM: Coming, Pa! I have to go now, Mr. Crankcase. Mr. Crankcase? Where are you? I wonder where everyone goes? *(Exit* HAM.*)*

WALTER *(from offstage, in pain):* Time passes.

(PERSON *carrying sign "TIME" passes across the stage. Enter* WALTER.)

* * * OPTIONAL SCENE * * *

(At this point you could skip a couple of pages for the sake of time or effort. This would cause very little loss in the story's continuity.)

WALTER: After the ark was finished, each of the sons had a job to do.

(*Enter* HAM *with rolled-up scroll.*)

WALTER: Ham, what is your special job?

HAM: Duh, I am getting all of the little animals together.

WALTER: Good. How are you doing?

HAM: Very well, thank you. Pa has given me a list, and I check off each little animal that we load. Do you want to hear what we have? (HAM *unrolls list, which goes across the stage.*)

WALTER: I don't think we have ... (*As* HAM *reads the list,* WALTER *pushes him offstage.*)

HAM: There is the cute little aardvark, and the scaly ol' alligator, and the itty-bitty ants, and bushy-tailed anteaters, and the pretty little antelope, and the funny-faced apes . . . *(Exit)*

WALTER *(deep breath)*: Well, let's see how Shem is doing.

(Enter SHEM with a scroll of his own.)

SHEM: What a pain!

WALTER: What's the problem, Shem?

SHEM: I have to get all the food together.

WALTER: That would be a big job. You folks will probably be on that ark for a long time.

SHEM: It's not just us, but the animals too!

WALTER: That's a lot of work!

SHEM: You bet. *(Unrolls scroll across the stage)* I've got to get hay for the horsies, and bananas for the monkeys, and honey for the bears . . .

WALTER: Oh, no. Not again.

(WALTER starts to push SHEM offstage as he continues to read his list, when from the opposite direction HAM comes back reading his list.)

SHEM: And cheese for the mousies . . .

HAM: . . . and I've got little bunny rabbits . . .

SHEM: . . . and nuts for the squirrels . . .

WALTER *(finally pushing SHEM offstage)*: We've got plenty of nuts! *(Pushes HAM offstage)*

HAM *(as he exits)*: . . . And I've got Santa's reindeer . . .

WALTER *(breathing hard)*: Let's see what Japheth is up to. *(Enter JAPHETH, holding his own list.)*

JAPHETH: Women!

WALTER: What's wrong, Japheth?

JAPHETH: Well, I'm in charge of loading everything onto the ark. I have to find a place for each item and animal.

WALTER: So you have some big problems.

JAPHETH: Well, actually, it's going fairly well. Except when Ham keeps putting the hamsters next to the pythons. We've had to restock our hamsters five times, and our pythons are slightly overweight.

WALTER: Superbrain strikes again.

JAPHETH: The real problem is the people. With all these animals and things, there's not going to be much room for our things.

WALTER: Only the bare essentials, right?

JAPHETH: Right, but some people don't know what bare essentials are.

(Enter MRS. NOAH, *carrying hair dryer behind her.*)

MRS. NOAH: Oh, Japheth!

JAPHETH (*to* WALTER): Watch; you'll see what I mean.

MRS. NOAH: Japheth, dear, I was wondering if you could squeeze this itty-bitty thing into the ark. (*Holds up hair dryer*)

JAPHETH: Mom, how many times do I have to tell you, only the very, very important things go!

WALTER: Yes, ma'am. Only the bare essentials.

MRS. NOAH (*to* WALTER): Keep out of this, nosy. (*To* JAPHETH) Now, dear, you know how much I need my hair dryer—

JAPHETH: No, Mom.

MRS. NOAH (*moves closer to* JAPHETH): My Vegamatic vegetable slicer?

JAPHETH: No, Mom.

MRS. NOAH (*right next to* JAPHETH): My electric toothbrush?

JAPHETH: No, Mom.

MRS. NOAH (*right on top of* JAPHETH): MY MOUTHWASH!

JAPHETH: That you can take. Go finish packing, Mom.

MRS. NOAH (*resigned*): So, what's to pack? (*Exit*)

WALTER: Boy, you've really got to be rough!

JAPHETH: That's right, or there wouldn't be room for the important stuff like . . . (*unrolls his list*) . . . my skateboard . . .

WALTER: Your what??

JAPHETH: . . . and my boogie board . . . (*Starts to exit*) . . . and my baseball card collection . . .

WALTER: Oh, brother.

JAPHETH (*exits*): . . . and my Monopoly game . . .

WALTER: While his sons were taking care of their chores, Noah was having to deal with his neighbors. And they weren't very nice.

※ ※ ※ OPTIONAL SCENE ENDS HERE ※ ※ ※

(At this point you would start again if you were eliminating the middle section of dialogue.)

(Enter NOAH.)

NOAH: I sure hope it starts raining soon.

WALTER: Are you through with the ark, Noah?

NOAH: Sure. We're loading the last of the food and animals right now.

WALTER: Then what's the problem?

NOAH: My neighbors. I'm getting a little tired of their smart remarks.

WALTER: Like what?

(Enter HECKLER 1 *and* HECKLER 2.)

NOAH: You'll see.

HECKLER 1: Hey, Noah! I thought I saw you load an elephant on this thing. But I guess I was wrong. It was your wife!

(HECKLERS *laugh.*)

HECKLER 2: Hey, Noah! That's a real nice boat you've got there. You forgot one thing, though: the water!

(HECKLERS *laugh.*)

HECKLER 1: That's one ugly-looking boat you have there, Noah. You'd better shape it up or ship it out!

(HECKLERS *laugh.*)

NOAH *(to* WALTER): See what I mean by smart remarks?

WALTER *(shaking head):* Those don't sound too smart to me.

HECKLER 2: We'd better be careful, or Noah's big, bad God might do something nasty to us.

HECKLER 1: Ooooo! I'm scared!

(HECKLERS *laugh. Thunder sounds.* HECKLERS *stop laughing and look around.)*

HECKLER 2: You don't suppose . . .

HECKLER 1: Nah, it couldn't be . . .

HECKLER 2: I wonder. Has anyone invented life jackets yet?

(Exit HECKLERS.*)*

NOAH *(holding hand out as if to feel the rain):* Well, I'd better get aboard. It looks like we're about to sail. *(Exit)*

(Thunder. Lightning. Rain. Wind.)

WALTER *(to audience):* So the great Flood started. Time passes.

*(*PERSON*, wearing a scuba mask, carrying sign "TIME," passes across the stage.)*

WALTER: Noah really had to trust God. His ark just floated wherever the wind would blow, so Noah had no idea where he was.

(Enter NOAH*, hopefully in a sailing cap.)*

NOAH: Well, that's not quite true. Through my navigational skills, using the stars for my position, my modern compass for my bearing, the position of the sun at noon, and (most important) *(holds up map)* my Automobile Club map, I have a pretty good idea where I am.

WALTER *(looking at map):* I don't see how a map of Tulsa, Okla., would help you, but why don't you tell me where you are?

NOAH *(glancing at map and then at sky):* I am standing right here on the deck of my boat . . . drifting somewhere . . . in the middle of nowhere.

WALTER *(sarcastically):* Brilliant.

NOAH: I better call a meeting of my crew. All hands on deck!!

(Enter SHEM, HAM, *and* JAPHETH. *Any sailing clothes will do.)*

NOAH: OK, boys, let's see if we can figure out where we are.

*(*NOAH *and* SONS *huddle together, making different remarks like:)*
    . . . I think we're 200 miles due west . . . or is it east?
    . . . We turned left at that last wave.
    . . . Didn't we just pass Lompoc?
    . . . Why don't we stop at a filling station and ask?
    . . . I thought I saw a policeman at that last intersection.
    . . . It's 2:30, so we must be near Tampa.

(A mountain peak creeps up—and "drifts" toward the boat.)

WALTER *(seeing mountain):* Uh, fellows . . .

*(*NOAH *keeps talking.)*

WALTER: Guys, there's a—

(*"Smash" into mountain.* NOAH *and* SONS *fall to the floor in a pile, with* NOAH *on the bottom.*)

HAM: Duh . . . Pa, that's a mountain.

NOAH (*straining from under pile*): Thank you, Son.

SHEM (*panicked, but not moving off* NOAH): We crashed!! Get off the ship!

JAPHETH: We can't swim!!

SHEM: Oh.

HAM (*also panicked*): We're sinking!! Get into the lifeboats!!

SHEM: We don't have any lifeboats!

HAM: Oh.

JAPHETH: We're lost!! Get on your life jackets!!

HAM: We don't got none!

JAPHETH: Oh.

NOAH (*exasperated*): WE'RE STUCK!! GET OFF MY BACK!!

SHEM, HAM, and JAPHETH: Oh.

(*They unpile.*)

HAM: What are we gonna do, Pa?

NOAH: We're going to wait right here until the water is gone.

JAPHETH: Good thing I brought my Monopoly game.

SHEM: After 250 games of Monopoly, it gets a little boring.

HAM: I wonder what mountain this is anyway.

(*A sign pops up from behind the mountain, saying "Mount Ararat."*)

HAM: Duh . . . thank you.

WALTER (*to audience*): So there Noah and his sons sat, stuck on Mount Ararat as time passed.

(PERSON *carrying sign "TIME" passes across the stage.* NOAH *and* SONS *watch him closely.*)

SHEM: Tough job.

JAPHETH: He doesn't have many lines, does he?

(*Exit* HAM.)

WALTER: Noah tested to see if the water had left the earth. First, he sent out a raven, but it never came back. Then he sent out a dove. It returned to the boat twice, but the second time . . .

(Enter HAM with huge branch.)

HAM: Hey, Pa! Look what the little birdie brought back.

JAPHETH: That must be one strong little birdie.

NOAH: Boys! This means that the water is almost all gone from the earth!

HAM: Oh, boy. I'll go tell Ma!

(HAM swings around and hits one or more of the other characters with the branch and exits.)

SHEM: We better get out of here soon, or we might not survive.

WALTER: When Noah sent out the dove the third time, it didn't come back.

NOAH *(to SHEM and JAPHETH)*: Sons. This means that the water is gone. But we still must wait for God to tell us to leave the boat.

(Enter HAM with telephone.)

HAM: Pa, it's for you.

NOAH: Yes, Lord. . . . Right, Lord. . . . Thank You very much. . . . Good-bye. *(Hangs up)* We can leave!

SHEM, HAM, and JAPHETH: Yeah!!

SHEM *(pointing to sky)*: Hey, Dad, what's that thing up in the sky?

JAPHETH: It sure is pretty.

HAM: Look at all the colors.

NOAH: That's God's promise that He will never destroy the earth by flood again. Let's go out and build an altar and thank God for saving us.

JAPHETH: That's a great idea.

SHEM: Last one out cleans up the ark!

(NOAH and SONS push and shove as they run to exit.)

WALTER: And that's the way it was, for Noah and his family. This is Walter Crankcase thanking you, and saying—*(stops suddenly)*—hold on a second . . . I'm going to be the last one here! *(Running off to exit)* Wait a minute! I'm not cleaning up this thing!

(Music. PERSON who carried "TIME" sign comes through with sign that says, "THE END." Music fades.)